W9-ADL-582

GRAPHIC LIBRARY™

INVENTIONS AND DISCOVERY

LOUIS PASTEUR and PASTEURIZATION

by Jennifer Fandel

illustrated by Keith Wilson, Rodney Ramos, and Charles Barnett III

Consultant:
Harry W. Paul
Professor Emeritus of History
University of Florida
Gainesville, Florida

Capstone

Mankato, Minnesota

Graphic Library is published by Capstone Press,
151 Good Counsel Drive, P.O. Box 669, Mankato, Minnesota 56002.
www.capstonepress.com

1 2 3 4 5 6 12 11 10 09 08 07

Library of Congress Cataloging-in-Publication Data
Fandel, Jennifer.
    Louis Pasteur and pasteurization / by Jennifer Fandel; illustrated by Keith Wilson,
Rodney Ramos, and Charles Barnett III.
        p. cm.—(Graphic library: Inventions and discovery)
    Includes bibliographical references and index.
    ISBN-13: 978-0-7368-6844-0 (hardcover)
    ISBN-10: 0-7368-6844-5 (hardcover)
    ISBN-13: 978-0-7368-7896-8 (softcover pbk.)
    ISBN-10: 0-7368-7896-3 (softcover pbk.)
    1. Pasteur, Louis, 1822–1895—Comic books, strips, etc. 2. Microbiologists—France—
Biography—Comic books, strips, etc. 3. Food—Pasteurization—Comic books, strips, etc. I.
Wilson, Keith, 1936– ill. II. Ramos, Rodney, ill. III. Barnett, Charles, III ill. IV. Title. V. Series.
QR31.P37F36 2007
579.092—dc22
[B]   2006031540

Summary: In graphic novel format, tells the story of Louis Pasteur's invention of the
    pasteurization process and the effects of this invention on the spread of disease
    through food.

Designer Alison Thiele	*Colorist* Tami Collins
Storyboard Artist Ron Frenz	*Editor* Gillia Olson

Editor's note: Direct quotations from primary sources are indicated by a yellow background.

Direct quotations appear on the following pages:

Page 10, from the Oxford Dictionary of Quotations (New York: Oxford University Press, 1999).
Page 11, quoted in *Louis Pasteur* by Patrice Debre (Baltimore: Johns Hopkins University
    Press, 1998).

TABLE OF CONTENTS

CHAPTER 1
HAZARDOUS FOOD

In the mid-1800s, people didn't know that germs cause disease. They knew microorganisms existed, but they were believed to be harmless. Because no one knew that germs cause disease, no one knew how diseases spread.

Pierre has the beginning stages of a disease called tuberculosis, but he wouldn't think to wash his hand after coughing into it.

COUGH!
COUGH!

He doesn't realize that his unwashed hand sent thousands of tiny germs into the milk he gathered from the family cow.

People in the 1800s saw illness as a part of life. Many believed that evil spirits caused disease.

Countless people died from disease carried in unsafe food.

But things were changing. In the mid-1800s, French chemist Louis Pasteur began to research food spoilage. Slowly, the mysterious connection between food and disease-causing germs would be uncovered.

CHAPTER 2
A LIVING PROCESS

In 1854, Pasteur was the head of a college in Lille, France. His job led him to research problems occurring in the community. In 1856, he visited Mr. Bigo, a beet alcohol producer with a spoilage problem.

My beet alcohol is ruined. The beets are fine, but the alcohol keeps spoiling.

May I take some samples of the alcohol? Both good and bad batches?

Of course.

Back at his lab, Pasteur looked at the samples under a microscope.

Interesting.

Pasteur wondered if microorganisms always grew so easily. In his studies during 1860, he opened sealed flasks of liquid in different places to see if different conditions, such as temperature, affected the growth of microorganisms.

Warm, moist conditions seem to encourage growth.

Hot, dry conditions keep growth down.

And cold nearly stops growth.

From these studies, Pasteur hoped to disprove the theory of spontaneous generation. Many scientists believed that microorganisms came from a mysterious "life force" in the air.

The swan-necked shape should trap germs in the bends but still allow air into the flask.

CHAPTER 3
FROM PROBLEM TO PROCESS

In 1861, Pasteur won the Zecker Prize from the Academy of Sciences in Paris for disproving spontaneous generation. After winning the award, Pasteur was asked by France's king, Napoleon III, to help France's wine industry. France exported a lot of wine to other countries, but it often arrived spoiled.

Are there any problems with your grapes?

No. They look and taste like they always do.

Pasteur and his assistants tried his new machine.

It works! Brilliant job, all of you.

He then showed winemakers how to build or modify their own equipment into pasteurization machines.

Some French winemakers still weren't convinced to use pasteurization.

Heating wine! Who ever heard of such a thing?

The wine tastes terrible!

Winemaking is an art. A scientist cannot tell us what to do.

Other winemakers immediately adopted the process. Still, pasteurization was slow to catch on in other industries.

CHAPTER 4
PASTEURIZATION FOR HEALTH

Louis Pasteur's work with germs made him an early supporter of the germ theory of disease. Soon, new discoveries about germs would give pasteurization a new purpose.

In 1882, Robert Koch made a startling announcement.

I have identified the tuberculosis bacteria and proven that it causes the disease.

Today, pasteurization continues to make milk safe to drink. Thanks to the work of Louis Pasteur in the 1800s, people became more aware of the science behind our food supply.

MORE ABOUT
LOUIS PASTEUR and
PASTEURIZATION

 Louis Pasteur was born in 1822 in France. He died in 1895. At the time of his death, he was considered a hero in France. The government ordered a state funeral, an honor usually given to a country's president or king. Many citizens joined the funeral procession in the streets of Paris.

 Pasteur and his wife Marie had five children, but only two lived past childhood. Two died of typhoid, a disease that attacks the intestines, while an unknown disease struck the other child. The deaths of his children motivated Pasteur to study diseases and learn to prevent them.

 Pasteur was very protective of his work. Even on vacation, Pasteur took his notebooks that contained the details of his experiments with him. He kept extremely detailed notes, numbering around 10,000 pages.

 Pasteurization helps kill bacteria that can show up in milk supplies. Some of the deadly diseases it can prevent are typhoid fever, tuberculosis, scarlet fever, and polio.

Milk isn't the only pasteurized food. Apple cider, juices, water, and some canned goods are often pasteurized.

Since Pasteur's experiments with pasteurization, food scientists have tried different methods to keep foods safe to eat. For drinks that may be stored on shelves and refrigerated after opening, flash pasteurization is usually used. This type of pasteurization uses very high temperatures for a short time.

Pasteur's germ research took him from pasteurization to discoveries about fighting diseases with vaccines. He developed vaccines for rabies and anthrax.

GLOSSARY

bacteria (bak-TIHR-ee-uh)—microscopic living things; some bacteria cause disease.

germ (JURM)—a microorganism; people usually use the word "germs" for microorganisms that make people sick.

microorganism (mye-kro-OR-gan-iz-um)—a living thing too small to be seen without a microscope

patent (PAT-uhnt)—a legal document that gives an inventor the right to make, use, or sell an invention for a set number of years

tuberculosis (tu-BUR-kyoo-low-sis)—a disease caused by bacteria that causes fever, weight loss, and coughing; left untreated, tuberculosis can lead to death.

yeast (YEEST)—a kind of microorganism called a fungus that causes dough to rise and alcohol to form

INTERNET SITES

FactHound offers a safe, fun way to find Internet sites related to this book. All of the sites on FactHound have been researched by our staff.

Here's how:
1. Visit *www.facthound.com*
2. Choose your grade level.
3. Type in this book ID **0736868445** for age-appropriate sites. You may also browse subjects by clicking on letters, or by clicking on pictures and words.
4. Click on the **Fetch It** button.

FactHound will fetch the best sites for you!

READ MORE

Fullick, Ann. *Louis Pasteur.* Groundbreakers. Chicago: Heinemann, 2001.

Isle, Mick. *Everything You Need to Know about Food Poisoning.* The Need to Know Library. New York: Rosen, 2001.

Nye, Bill. *Bill Nye the Science Guy's Great Big Book of Tiny Germs.* New York: Hyperion Books for Children, 2005.

Solway, Andrew. *What's Living in Your Kitchen?* Hidden Life. Chicago: Heinemann, 2004.

BIBLIOGRAPHY

Conant, James Bryant, ed. *Pasteur's Study of Fermentation.* Harvard Case Studies in Experimental Science. Cambridge, Mass.: Harvard University Press, 1952.

Debré, Patrice. *Louis Pasteur.* Baltimore: Johns Hopkins University Press, 1998.

Geison, Gerald L. *The Private Science of Louis Pasteur.* Princeton, N.J.: Princeton University Press, 1995.

Hall, Carl W., and G. Malcolm Trout. *Milk Pasteurization.* Westport, Conn.: Avi Publishing, 1968.

INDEX